A Day in the Life of an...

Ambulance Team

Carol Watson

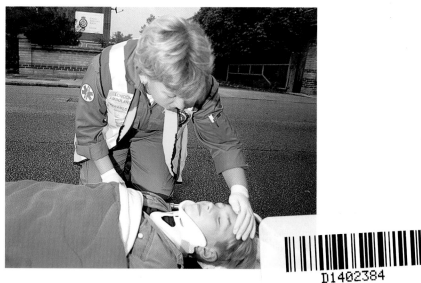

W
FRANKLIN WATTS
NEW YORK • LONDON • SYDNEY

Jacqui and Ennio work together as an ambulance team. They are one of many teams based at a large ambulance station.

The team start
their shift by
checking over
their vehicle.
"I'll have a look
at the oil level,"
says Jacqui.

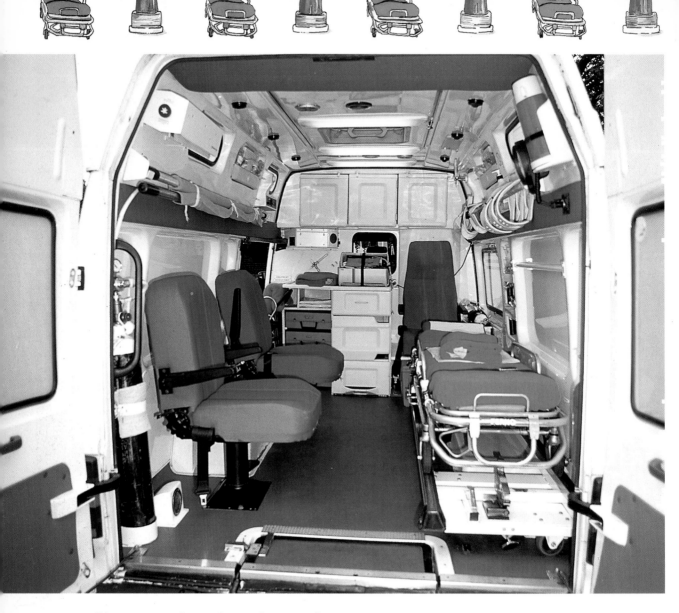

Ennio checks that there is
enough petrol and looks
inside the ambulance to see
that everything is in order.

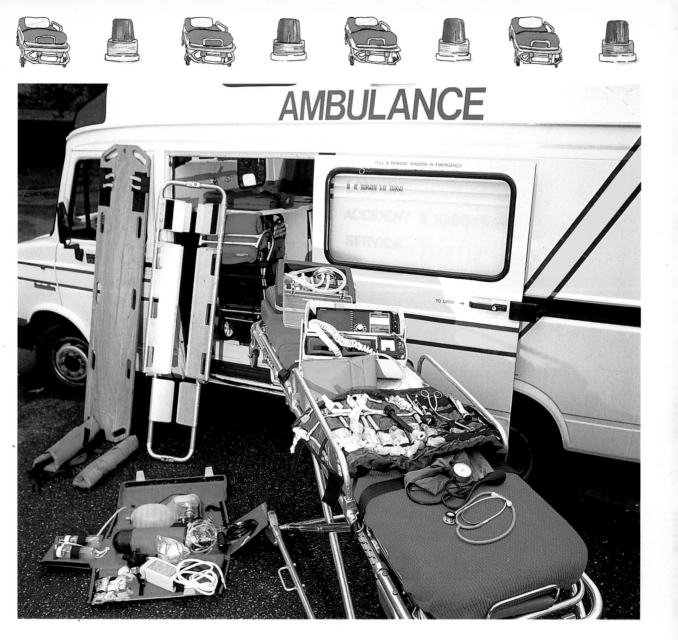

Every ambulance carries
equipment to help sick or
injured people. This includes
oxygen to help them breathe.

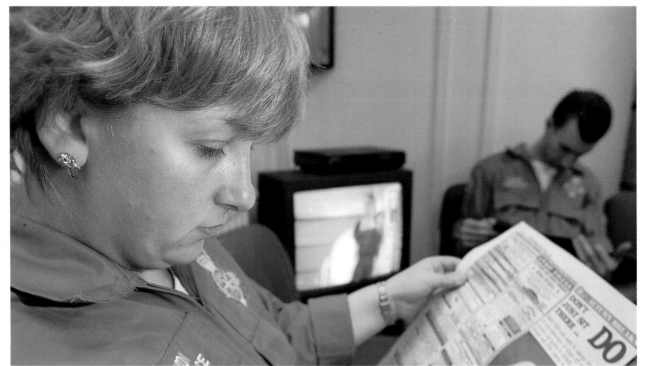

Jacqui and Ennio
wait in the Mess
Room until they
are needed.
The telephone rings.
Ennio takes the call
and writes down
the details.

"It's an accident in Spring Road,"
he tells Jacqui. They quickly
climb into the ambulance. Jacqui
speaks to Control on the radio.

"Foxtrot 201 to Control," says Jacqui, using the code for her station.
She checks the details, as Ennio speeds through the busy traffic.

The ambulance arrives at the scene.

Edward has been knocked over and lies injured in the road.

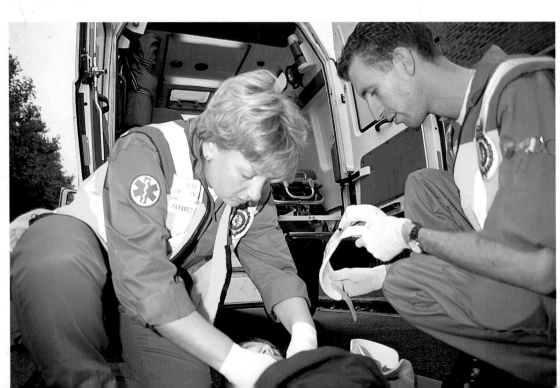

The team quickly go into action.
They check the boy's airway, breathing and pulse. This tells them how seriously he is hurt.

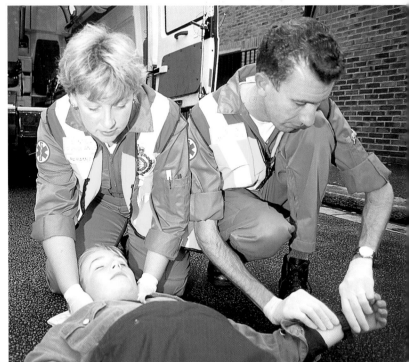

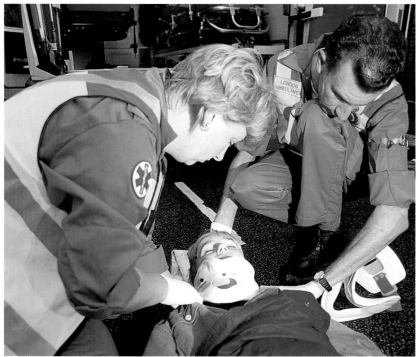

Next they put on a collar to stop the patient moving his head and neck.

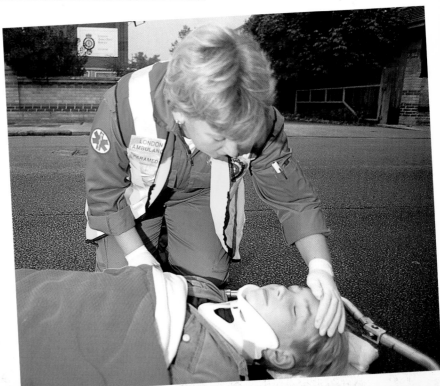

"Can you hear me Edward?" Jacqui asks the boy.

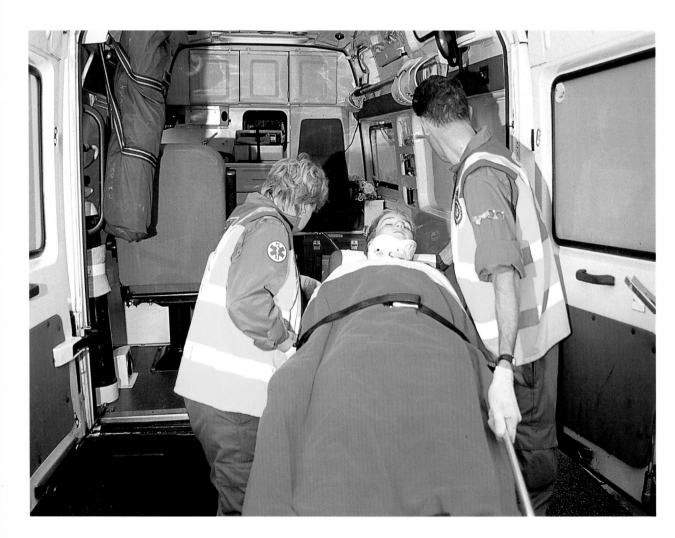

The team carefully lift the
stretcher onto the ambulance.
Jacqui climbs in the back
to look after the patient.

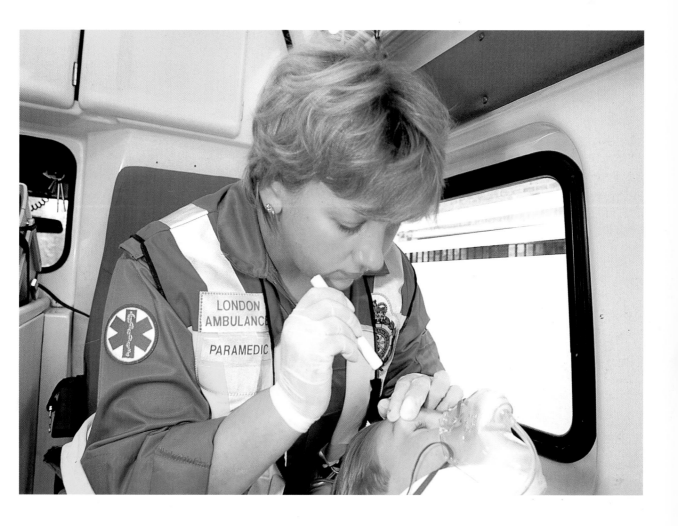

Ennio puts on the siren as he
drives Edward to hospital.
Jacqui watches the boy's
eye movements with her torch.

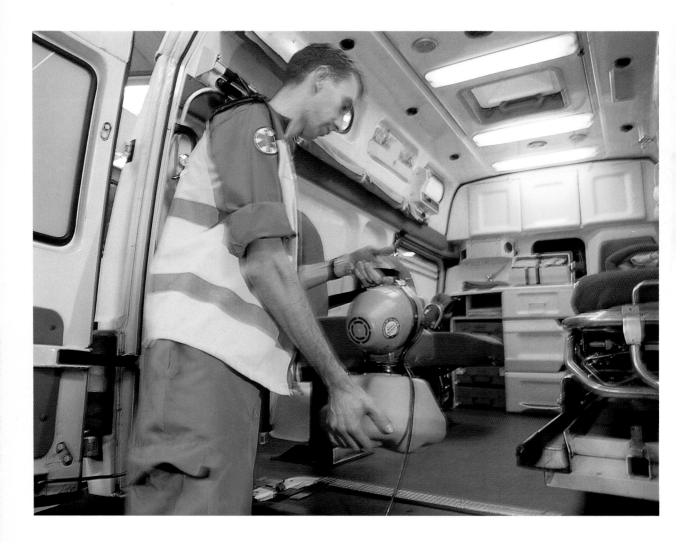

Once Edward is safely in hospital, the team return to their base. Ennio uses a machine to disinfect the ambulance.

As they wait for their next call, Jacqui and Ennio have a tea break. Then the telephone rings again. "I'll get it," says Ennio.

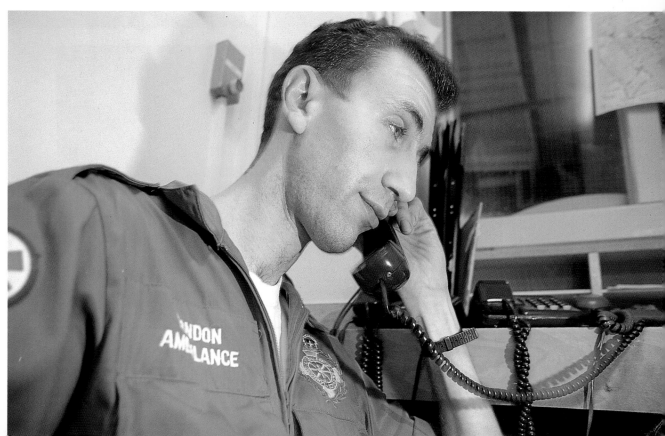

Jan is having an asthma attack.

Ennio takes her pulse to see how quickly her heart is beating.

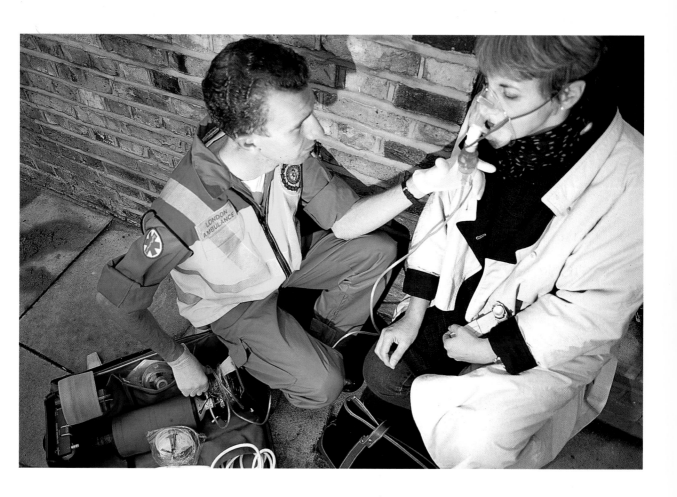

"This will help you to breathe,"
says Ennio. He puts a mask
over Jan's face so she can
breathe in oxygen.

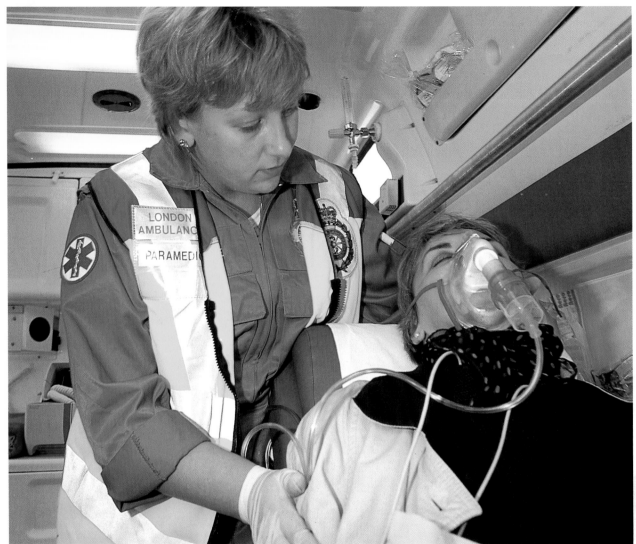

As Ennio drives the ambulance,
Jacqui talks quietly to Jan.
"Don't worry," she says.
"We're nearly at the hospital."

At the end of their shift, Jacqui writes down all that has happened.

It's time for the ambulance team to go home.

Take your own pulse

You will need: a watch or clock with a second hand, or a
timer that tells you when one minute is over.

When the ambulance team take someone's pulse, they are
checking how quickly the patient's heart is beating. You can
try this on yourself and your friends.

   The best place for you to feel your pulse is on the side of
your neck, near your 'Adam's apple'.

1. Very gently, put your fingers
   on the side of your neck until
   you can feel a movement
   inside your throat. You will
   feel it beating quite quickly.

2. Set your timer to 0, or
   wait until the second
   hand of your watch
   reaches 12.

3. Count how many beats you can feel before the second hand reaches 12 again, or one minute is up on your timer.

4. Write down how many beats you counted.

Now go for a run round your garden, or up and down some stairs. Come back and take your pulse again. Write down how many beats to a minute there are this time.

Is there a difference?
Try it out on your friends and family and see what happens.

Your pulse might be anything between 80-160 beats a minute.

How you can help Ambulance Teams

1. Always be careful crossing the road. Try to use a Zebra or Pelican Crossing. Use the Green Cross Code. Look all around before you cross.

2. Never play in the road.

3. Always wear your seat belt in both the back and front of a car or minibus.

4. Be careful when you are getting out of a car. Always get out on the side of the pavement.

5. If you see someone lying on the ground hurt, don't move them. Put a coat or blanket over them to keep them warm.

Dial 999 and ask for an ambulance. Make sure you tell the operator where you are and what is happening.

Facts about the Ambulance Service

An ambulance team is made up of a driver and an attendant. In this book, Ennio, the driver, is a Qualified Ambulance Person (Q.A.P), and Jacqui, the attendant, is a Paramedic.

The calls come to the ambulance station from Ambulance Control. Each station and its vehicles have code numbers. The Control contacts them by telephone or radio.

The calls received by the Control are sorted out into those that are most urgent. Accident calls are usually answered before all the others. The ambulance goes to the scene immediately.

Only in a real emergency will the ambulance use a siren.

Helicopters, motor cycles and **transport vehicles** are also used by the ambulance service.

Index

© 1995 Franklin Watts

Franklin Watts
96 Leonard Street
London
EC2A 4XD

Franklin Watts Australia
14 Mars Road
Lane Cove
NSW 2066

ISBN: 0 7496 1997 X (hb)
     0 7496 3635 1 (pb)

Dewey Decimal Classification
Number: 362.1

10 9 8 7 6 5 4 3 2 1

A CIP catalogue record for
this book is available from the
British Library.

Printed in Malaysia

Editor: Sarah Ridley
Designer: Nina Kingsbury
Photographer: Chris Honeywell
Illustrations: Michael Evans

With thanks to:
Station Commander Bob Dobson,
Jacqui Mee, Ennio Tabone and the
services of Fulham Ambulance
Station; Victoria and Edward
Wethered, Mr Jeremy Booth.